NUESTRAS COMUNIDADES
AMERICAN COMMUNITIES

Vivimos en un **pueblo**

—

We Live in a **Small Town**

Mary Austen

Traducido por Esther Sarfatti

PowerKiDS press

New York

Published in 2016 by The Rosen Publishing Group, Inc.
29 East 21st Street, New York, NY 10010

Copyright © 2016 by The Rosen Publishing Group, Inc.

All rights reserved. No part of this book may be reproduced in any form without permission in writing from the publisher, except by a reviewer.

First Edition

Editor: Katie Kawa
Book Design: Reann Nye
Traducido por: Esther Sarfatti

Photo Credits: Cover, p. 21 Kenneth Sponsler/Shutterstock.com; cover, pp. 3–24 (background texture) Evgeny Karandaev/Shutterstock.com; p. 5 Tom Merton/Caiaimage/Getty Images; p. 6 (town) Sean Doug Schneider Photography/Moment/Getty Images; pp. 6 (city), 13 littleny/Shutterstock.com; p. 9 Michael Shake/Shutterstock.com; pp. 10, 24 (post office) Joseph Sohm/Shutterstock.com; p. 14 (top) Pressmaster/Shutterstock.com; p. 14 (bottom) wavebreakmedia/Shutterstock.com; p. 17 Flashon Studio/ Shutterstock.com; pp. 18, 24 (town hall) DonLand/Shutterstock.com; p. 22 Sergey Novikov/Shutterstock.com; p. 24 (library) DavidPinoPhotography/Shutterstock.com.

Cataloging-in-Publication Data

Austen, Mary.
 We live in a small town = Vivimos en un pueblo / Mary Austen.
    pages cm. — (American Communities = Nuestras comunidades)
Parallel title: Nuestras comunidades.
In English and Spanish.
Includes webography.
Includes index.
ISBN 978-1-5081-4734-3 (library binding)
1. Cities and towns—Juvenile literature. I. Title.
HT119.A97 2016
307.76—dc23

Manufactured in the United States of America

CPSIA Compliance Information: Batch #BW16PK: For Further Information contact Rosen Publishing, New York, New York at 1-800-237-9932

Contenido
Contents

Un pueblo es un lugar estupendo para vivir.

A small town is a great place to live.

5

pueblo
town

ciudad
city

6

Un pueblo es un tipo de comunidad urbana. Un pueblo es como una ciudad, pero más pequeño.

A town is a kind of urban community. A town is like a city, but it is smaller.

Muchos de los edificios de nuestro pueblo están en la misma calle. Esta calle se llama la Calle Principal.

Many of the buildings in our town are on the same street. This street is called Main Street.

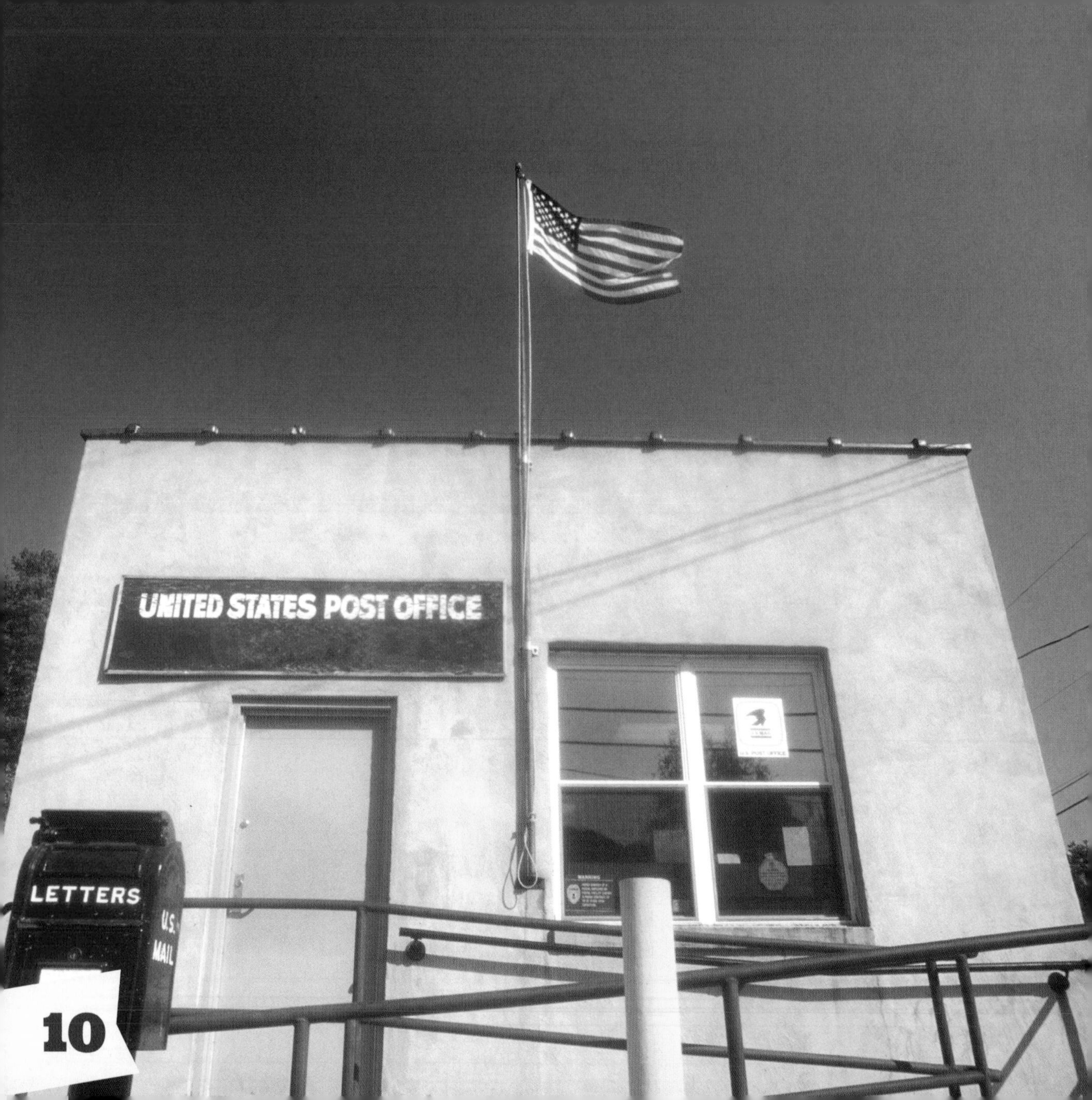
UNITED STATES POST OFFICE
LETTERS
U.S. MAIL

Nuestra **oficina de correos** está en la Calle Principal. Vamos allí si queremos enviar una carta.

Our **post office** is on Main Street. This is where we go to send letters.

Todos los niños de nuestro pueblo van a la misma escuela.

All the kids in our town go to the same school.

13

Algunos niños van andando a la escuela. Otros toman el autobús.

Some kids walk to school. Some kids ride the bus.

Nuestro pueblo tiene una **biblioteca**. Allí se pueden tomar prestados libros, películas y música.

Our small town has one **library**. This is a place to borrow books, movies, and music.

17

Nuestro alcalde es el que dirige nuestro pueblo. El alcalde trabaja en el **ayuntamiento**.

Our mayor is the leader of our town. The mayor works at the **town hall**.

En nuestro pueblo hay más árboles y plantas que en una gran ciudad.

Our town has more trees and plants than a big city.

En nuestro pueblo tenemos un parque. ¡Es un lugar divertido para jugar con los amigos!

We have a park in our small town. It is a fun place to play with friends!

Palabras que debes aprender
Words to Know

(la) biblioteca
library

(la) oficina
de correos
post office

(el) ayuntamiento
town hall

Índice / Index

Sitios de internet / Websites

Due to the changing nature of Internet links, PowerKids Press has developed an online list of websites related to the subject of this book. This site is updated regularly. Please use this link to access the list: www.powerkidslinks.com/acom/smtwn